'Paul Delaney goes on and on!' (Anon)

First published in October 2015 by FeedARead.com

Second edition published in August 2016

Text © Paul Delaney

Illustrations © Danny Long

Design © The Pig tourist publishing

A CIP catalogue record for this title is available from the British Library.

www.pdelaney.co.uk

Other books by Paul Delaney:

(All available in paperback / kindle download)

Sparrowlegs

I'm fed up! (poetry)

My toilet is a murderer!

The magical Madame Mistral

My favourite trainers (poetry)

Coming soon:

Norris Snoot

Gracie Blunkett and the Prince Oddie golden sock

Paul Delaney is a poet, a writer and a professional organist. He spends his time writing stories and poems and playing the organ and piano. Paul enjoys visiting schools across the U.K., developing children's love of modern poetry and creative writing. However, he's now in great demand as a school dinner tester...

Paul has three cool and trendy boys called Harry, George and Freddie. They're all super sporty too but Paul wasn't. He once turned up at a school rugby match wearing ice skates and carrying a snooker cue.

www.pdelaney.co.uk

Danny Long also lives in Widnes, where he likes to draw funny pictures and ride his bicycle but not at the same time. He also likes drinking tea and sometimes drinks 100 mugs a day – but not always with biscuits!

Danny was once in Paul's class in Y4. He loved this as he was allowed to draw and paint silly pictures whilst everybody else worked on their English and Maths!

www.danny-long.com

With thanks to the staff & children of the following schools, who heard these poems first!

St Joseph's Catholic Primary School,
Pontefract, West Yorkshire

Holy Family and St Michael's Catholic Primary School,
Pontefract, West Yorkshire

Penketh South Primary School,
Warrington, Cheshire

Trinity Catholic Primary School,
Liverpool, Merseyside

Brooklands Primary School
Blackheath, London

The Dingle Primary School,
Haslington, Cheshire

St Albert's Catholic Primary School,
Liverpool, Merseyside

Saughall All Saints C of E Primary School
Saughall, Cheshire

Stamford Park Junior School
Altrincham, Cheshire

Our Lady of Perpetual Succour Catholic Primary School
Widnes, Cheshire

Hedgehogs 1

Big trucks 0

Paul Delaney

'Magic is believing in yourself.

If you can do that,
you can make anything happen..'

Johann Wolfgang Von Goethe

(1739 – 1832)

German poet

I can do this! Can you?

I can wiggle my toes.
Can you?

I can wiggle my toes and stretch my arms.
Can you?

I can wiggle my toes, stretch my arms
and pull a funny face.
Can you?

I can wiggle my toes, stretch my arms,
pull a funny face and dance my legs.
All at the same time!
Can you?

I can wiggle my toes, stretch my arms,
pull a funny face, dance my legs
and move my head around.
All at the same time!
Can you?

I can wiggle my toes, stretch my arms,
pull a funny face, dance my legs,
move my head around
and bend my body like a banana.
All at the same time!
Can you?

I can wiggle my toes, stretch my arms,
pull a funny face, dance my legs,
move my head around,   .
bend my body like a banana
and scratch my head with my right hand.
All at the same time!
Can you?

I can wiggle my toes, stretch my arms,
pull a funny face, dance my legs,
move my head around,
bend my body like a banana,
scratch my head with my right hand
and make circles on my tummy with my left hand.
All at the same time!
Can you?

I can wiggle my toes, stretch my arms,
pull a funny face, dance my legs,
move my head around,
bend my body like a banana,
scratch my head with my right hand,
make circles on my tummy with my left hand
AND make the loudest,
silliest noise in the whole, wide world.
And all at the same time!
Can you?

If you can, you're FANTASTIC!

Because

I can't!

I love...

I love my mum
but she sometimes shouts at me!

I love my dad
but he often burns my tea!

I love my sister
but she's sometimes not my friend.

I love my brother
but he drives me round the bend!

I love my grandad
but his favourite word is 'NO!'

I love my Nana
but she always walks so slow.

I love my friends
but we're often falling out.

I love my teacher
but she has a nasty shout.

I love my dog,
but he chews and rips my shoe.

But I don't love one thing...

That's cleaning up his poo!

Just pretend!

Pretend you're a dinosaur!
Rah! Rah! Rah!
Stomp around the hall!
Rah! Rah! Rah!
Reach for the sky!
Rah! Rah! Rah!
Strong and tall!
Rah! Rah! Rah!

Pretend you're a baby!
Blah! Blah! Blah!
Cry for your mummy!
Blah! Blah! Blah!
Bang your spoon!
Blah! Blah! Blah!
Hungry tummy!
Blah! Blah! Blah!

Pretend you're a fire engine!
Wah! Wah! Wah!
Drive to a fire!
Wah! Wah! Wah!
Climb up ladders!
Wah! Wah! Wah!
Higher and higher!
Wah! Wah! Wah!

Pretend you're your mum!
Pretend you're your dad!
Pretend you're happy
and pretend you're sad.
Pretend you're a monster!
Pretend you're a tree!
Fall on the floor and
pretend to go asleep!

Mum said this!

'Look at the size of those checkout queues,'
Mum said.
'You'd think it was Christmas!'

'Let's use a self service machine,'
I said.
'There's no queue at that one.'

'Great idea, Isobel,'
Mum said.
'We'll scan this lot ourselves.'

'We'll save LOADS of time, Mum,'
I said.
'Come on, let's empty the trolley...'

Scan and bleep!
Scan and bleep!
Scan and bleep!
Scan and bleep!

Scan and bleep!
Scan and bleep!
Scan and bleep!
Scan and bleep!

**Unexpected
item
in
bagging
area!'**

Roses are red

Roses are red, violets are blue.
Ducks go quack and cows go moo.

Sheep go bleat and hens go cluck.
And pigs fall in love in mud and muck!

The sock monster

It's not in my drawer.
It's not in my wardrobe.
ONE of my socks, white and red.
It's not in the basket.
It's not on the floor.
It's definitely not under my bed.

It's not in the washer.
It's not in the drier.
It's not on my bedroom floor.
It's not in my pocket.
It's not in my school bag.
It's definitely no more.

The sock monster's ate it.
He's greedy and fat.
He's taking a hungry bite.
He's hiding in darkness.
He's lurking in shadows.
An expert at 'out of sight'.

He likes multi-colours
and different materials.
His favourites are football socks.
He creeps into rooms
in the middle of the night
a sly and cunning fox.

He roots through my drawers
and opens my wardrobe,
searching for precious prey.
One sock he steals,
from a fancied pair.
Before he slips away.

Into the night he disappears.
He's vanished in a tryst.
And I wake up in the morning,
searching for my socks missed...

£1000 reward for the

sock monster's capture!

Ask your mum!

'Dad, can I have another piece of cake?'

'Ask your mum!'

'Dad, can I go to Robyn's party on Saturday?'

'Ask your mum!'

'Dad, can I finish my homework tomorrow?'

'Ask your mum!'

'Dad, can I nip round to Olivia's?'

'Ask your mum!'

'Dad, can I stay up late tonight?'

'Ask your mum!'

'Mum, can I stay up late tonight?'

'Ask your dad!'

'Dad, can I stay up late tonight?'

'Ask your mum!'

'Mum, can I stay up late tonight?'

'Ask your dad!'

'Dad, can I stay up late tonight?'

'Ask your mum!'

'Mum, can I stay up late tonight?'

'NO - GET TO BED!'

Grandad Ken

He's waiting on the playground,
my grandad Ken.
He's hanging around,
a King amongst men.

Day after day,
he's right on time,
in all kinds of weather,
come rain or shine.

He takes me home
and we watch TV,
whilst Nanny's in the kitchen,
cooking our tea.

Three cheers for our grandparents,
who turn up at school,
dropping us off and picking us up,
now that's really cool!

Hip, hip! **Hooray!** (x3)

Hedgehogs 1
Big trucks 0

One baby hedgehog.
One busy road.
A thundering truck,
carrying its load.

The hedgehog steps out,
looking for a feed.
But the dangerous truck
increases its speed.

The merciless monster
ploughs through the smog,
running over Harold,
a helpless hedgehog.

But Harold's in luck,
he isn't under the wheels!
So he sprints out of danger,
towards green fields.

Hooray! A result!
The truck didn't kill.

Hedgehogs 1

Big Trucks 0

Toaster, toaster, burning bright!

Toaster, toaster, burning bright,
in the middle of the night.

Two rounds of bread, as white as snow,
heating up to a comforting glow.

'Pop up and spring!' your toast is done.
Your bread is scorched by electric sun.

Salted butter spread over your prize.
Watch it melt before your eyes.

Place your toast on a plate on your knee.
And enjoy your treat with a cup of tea.

Toaster, toaster, burning bright,
in the middle of the night.

Two rounds of bread, as white as snow,
heating up to a comforting glow.

Rainbow colours

Red is a juicy tomato,
yearning to be picked.

Orange is an ice-cold lolly ice,
hoping to be licked.

Yellow is a bowl of custard,
coating an apple pie.

Green is an ancient mountain,
stretching across the sky.

Blue is the colour of Everton,
Chelsea and Manchester City.

Indigo is a strange one,
a symbol of sorrow and pity.

Violet is a rare wild flower,
it's also a beautiful name.
It's sometimes the colour of toilet roll,
and that's a terrible shame!

My pen is running out!

'My pen is running out!'
shouted Aimee Lee McMearing.

'I'm trying to write my story
but my ink is disappearing!'

'How can your pen run out?'
cried the teacher, stamping her foot.

'You got a new one yesterday
and the door is firmly shut.'

Pens only run out when the classroom
door is open, so please beware, children!

Makes a Change!

Like a hedgehog on a zebra crossing.
Makes a change!

Like a dentist who forgets his flossing.
Makes a change!

Like a sergeant whispering not bossing.
Makes a change!

Like a painter spilling when he's glossing.
Makes a change!

Like a drifter working and not dossing.
Makes a change!

Like a pancake never ever tossing.
Makes a change!

Some things make a change!

One to ten

1 is an odd football sock,
its partner somewhere lost.

2 is a pair of woolly gloves,
   an extra skin in frost.

3 is a long, cardboard tube,
   of tennis balls, ready to play.

4 is a box of fresh cream cakes
   a treat at the end of the day.

5 is a flag of Olympic rings
   and bronze and silver and gold.

6 is a box of fresh hen's eggs,
from farm to market, sold.

7 are Snow White's happy dwarfs,
'hi-hoing' and working with glee.

8 are the legs of an octopus,

cutting through the sea.

9 are the forms of Chinese dragon,

breathing flames of fire.

10 is where this poem ends -

I'm not going any higher!

The seven wonders of Harry, George and Freddie's sporty world

1) Rugby league (HG)
2) Widnes RLFC (HG)
3) Halton hornets RLFC (HG)
4) Football (FG)
5) Widnes FC (FG)
6) Everton FC (F)
7) Wrestling (F)

KEY!

RLFC = Rugby league football club
FC = Football club
H = Harry
G = George
F = Freddie

Mother's day poem

Thank you Mum, for everything you do.
You're the best Mummy in the world!

You have super-charged legs and a soft
centred heart, a chocolate in a box.
You tidy my bedroom and drop me off at
school and even wash my socks.

You find things that I'd thought I'd lost.
How do you know where everything is?
If I was a bottle of cloudy lemonade,
you'd be the fruity fizz!

Thank you Mum, for everything you do.
You're the best Mummy in the world!

You do so many things for me,
so my poem could last forever.
I'm a happy child and happier still,
when we're doing stuff together.

I love you mummy and I always will!
The earth, the moon and the stars.
My love for you is longer still
than the miles from Mercury to Mars.

Thank you Mum, for everything you do.
You're the best Mummy in the world!

Father's day poem

My dad's SUPER and here's why:

SUPER Bananas and custard maker.
SUPER Pepperoni pizza cooker.
SUPER Silly joke teller.
SUPER Funny Face puller.
SUPER free taxi driver.
SUPER dishwasher emptier.
SUPER Rugby Union player.
SUPER caravan tower.
SUPER sports Gym goer.
SUPER maths homework solver.
SUPER sadness busting cuddler.

That's why you're SUPER!

And that's why I love you so much!

THANKS DAD xxxxxxx

The days of my week!

Monday is after school club day.
I'll play with Logan, Callum and Jenson.

(And I MIGHT play with Gracie and Scarlet!)

Tuesday is karate club day.
I'll karate chop Sensai when he's not looking!

Wednesday is Art and P.E. day.
I'll paint a picture and climb the monkey bars.
(Not at the same time though!)

Thursday is football training day.
I'll score a hat trick like Lionel Messi.

Friday is the best – Nanny and Grandad day.
I'll sit on Grandad's knee and watch TV.

Saturday is lie in bed for a bit day.
I'll cuddle my teddy bear and I'll fall back
asleep and I'll dream and dream and dream!

Sunday is rugby match day!
I'll score a try and win 'Man of the match'!
It's also Sunday roast day too!
I'll eat everything except sprouts!

What's in your week?

Vindaloo 3 My dad 0

The bathroom door opens.
My dad walks in.
He stares at me.
A trademark grin.

Dad sits on the toilet.
He does his business.
I think he's had a curry.
And three pints of Guinness.

Vindaloo's his favourite.
King prawns, filled with spice.
And marinated vegetables
with mountains of rice.

I can hear his bottom.
It's rudely blowing off.
Releasing the gases
from his Indian scoff.

'My bum's on fire!'
he cries in pain,
cursing Masalas
the Indian to blame.

He guzzles cold water,
ten gallons at least.
Reversing the effects
of his Indian feast.

But Dad's too late,
the damage is done.
His tummy is a battlefield
And the spices have won.

The bathroom door opens.
My dad walks out,
wondering what on earth
all the fuss is about.

But I know the score.
He's looking quite ill…

VINDALOO 3

MY DAD 0

The princess and the frog

In a woodland pond, a bullfrog rested,
on his favourite lily pad.
A princess appeared, heading for her castle,
her eyes all heavy and sad.

'I'm looking for love,' she said to the frog.
'I'm planning a spectacular marriage.
But I can't find a prince at the moment,
so I'm riding alone in my carriage.'

'It's your lucky day,' the frog remarked.
'Kiss me and then you'll see!'
But the princess didn't believe him,
despite his heartfelt plea.

'Kiss me please!' he shouted out.
'I'm a prince who's in disguise.'
But the beautiful princess turned away,
she thought he was telling lies.

*Sometimes, if we keep our eyes, ears and
hearts open, wonderful things can happen!*

But we have to believe in magic...

A happy smile

A happy smile goes a long, long way.
Brightening up somebody's day.

A laugh goes a whole lot further, of course
and pushes your troubles away!

Light your stars!

When I do something good,
a star is born in the sky.
But when I do something bad,
my star, it withers and dies.

Its light burns out for eternity.
Its spirit breathes its last.
It becomes a distant memory,
buried in my past.

So if you want a happy life,
full of dreams and wonder and love,
do many good deeds and light your stars,
in the heavens up above.

A birthday wish

A special day for you alone.
A wonderful child, it's true.
May happiness follow your footsteps
in whatever you choose to do.

Happy birthday my precious son.
Happy birthday my bundle of joy.
And may God protect you always,
my beautiful, talented boy.

A special day for you alone.
A wonderful child, it's true.
May happiness follow your footsteps
in whatever you choose to do.

Happy birthday my precious daughter.
Happy birthday, my whole wide world.
And may God protect you always,
my beautiful, talented girl.

Cows go moo!

Cows go **moo!**
Sheep go **baa!**
Dogs shove their heads out of **people's cars.**

Pigs go **oink!**
Hens go **cluck!**
Cats climb trees but often **get stuck!**

Birds go **tweet!**
Owls go **hoot!**
Hamsters store nuts and are **rather cute.**

Mums go **'NO!'**
Dads go **'Ask your mum!'**
And bees say nothing; they **simply hum.**

Follow your heart!

Follow your heart and not your head
and then your soul will sing.
Love and joy will be your friends,
if you trust your own inkling.

Swim with the current, not against the tide
and your spirit will soar and dance.
And a heavenly hand will be your guide
as long as you take that chance...

Hiding in the shadows...

Hiding in the shadows, a spider's asleep.
Patiently waiting: One, two, three.

He opens his eyes, which slowly peep.
Patiently waiting: One, two, three.

His sticky web stretches wide and deep.
Patiently waiting: One, two, three.

The spider explores, he starts to creep.
Patiently waiting: One, two, three.

His web vibrates under his feet.
Patiently waiting: One, two, three.

Alarm bells ring and buzzers bleep.
Patiently waiting: One, two, three.

A bluebottle's trapped, delicious meat.
Patiently waiting: One, two, three.

The spider scurries, towards his treat.
Patiently waiting: One, two, three.

The bluebottle's a black belt - an heroic feat.
Patiently waiting: One, two, three.

And karate chops the spider, off his seat.
Patiently waiting: One, two, three.

The spider falls, he's well and truly beat.
Patiently waiting: One, two, three.

And scours the ground for something to eat.
Patiently waiting: One, two, three.

Bluebottles One
Spiders Nil

(Sometimes, the underdog wins - hooray!)

Dance with me!

Dance with me and move your feet.
Feel the rhythm and feel the beat.
Open your eyes and look around.
Listen to happiness - what a sound!

Think of something that makes you sad.
NOW!

Think of something that makes you mad.
NOW!

Shout and sing 'It's a beautiful day!'
Let's dance those blues away!

Dance with me and move your feet.
Feel the rhythm and feel the beat.
Open your eyes and look around.
Listen to happiness - what a sound!

Shout 'Abracadabra' – banish your fears!
NOW!

Shout 'Bad things vanish and disappear!'
NOW!

Shout 'I believe in pixies, fairies and elves!'
NOW!

Think happy thoughts and powerful spells.
NOW!

Dance with me and move your feet.
Feel the rhythm and feel the beat.
Open your eyes and look around.
Listen to happiness - what a sound!

Peter's sister

Peter's sister woke up one day
and a tail was growing out of her bum.

'It's annoying me and I can't sit down!'
she shouted to her mum.

She chased a cat down Lovely Lane
and started to bark and woof.

But when she licked her best friend's face,
her dad said 'That's enough!'

Peter's mum googled the symptoms
on the high speed Internet.

And an online expert told her this –
take your daughter to a vet!

Wriggle your fingers!

Wriggle your fingers, pretend they're stars.
Dark, dark, **space.**

Move around, driving your cars!
Park, park, **space!**

Stretch your arms; pretend you're a tree.
Spring, summer, **fall.**

Fly around, buzzing like a bee.
Climb, dive, **fall.**

Sprint those legs; pretend you're a striker!
Match, goal, **ball.**

Dance around like Cinderella!
Pumpkin, Carriage, **ball.**

Open wide; pretend you're eating toast!
Butter, honey, **jam.**

Stop your car, driving to the coast.
Red, light, **jam.**

Stamp those feet; you're as tall as King Kong!
Stomp, roar, **duck.**

Pretend you're an otter in a river or a pond.
Swan, goose, **duck.**

You've probably noticed that all the words in bold have the same spelling but different meanings! They're called homophones.

Often, their spellings / meanings are different.

A witch **stirs** her bubbling cauldron

A cat **stares** at a startled mouse.

Quietly, a thief creeps up the **stairs.**

I know

I know a dentist
who doesn't brush his teeth.
He's always eating chocolate
and sugar coated sweets.
His teeth are falling out
and most of them are black.
He's not a proper dentist,
so he deserves the sack!

I know a vet
who never walks her dog.
She's always watching television,
eating like a hog.
Jasper's her terrier,
an energetic, playful breed.
But he's dreaming of the park
and a collar and a lead.

I know a teacher,
who doesn't mark her books.
She's always in the mirror,
admiring her looks.
Her children are complaining!
'Is it right or is it wrong?'
But Miss Wilkinson ticks everything,
which doesn't take her long!

I know a pilot,
who's terrified of heights.
He's flying Jumbo jets,
when he should be flying kites.
He's sitting in that cockpit,
with two trembling hands.
And he'll shake and shake
'til that aeroplane lands.

I know a zookeeper,
who never cleans out cages.
He simply sits around all day,
pretending to earn wages.
The lions are starving.
There's no meaty chunks to munch.
So when their lazy keeper arrives,
they gobble him up for lunch!

My mysterious moggy!

Where does my cat go
every single night?
For hours and hours,
he's out of my sight.

His fur is black
and he's difficult to see.
So as midnight strikes,
where on earth could he be?

I often wonder,
is he a witch's cat?
Her secret pet,
like a vampire bat?

Is he allowed
a broomstick ride?
Twisting and turning,
hover and glide.

Has he mixed
her potions and spells?
Stirring her cauldron,
bubbling smells.

Perhaps he wanders
for miles on Halloween?
Watching 'trick or treaters',
without being seen.

Every morning,
he creeps into my house.
And sometimes he's carrying
a little dead mouse.

But I'll never know
what his eyes have seen,
his night-time haunts,
the places he has been.

These are his secrets,
locked into his head,
like my secret money box,
hiding under my bed.
(Oh dear, I've told you where it is now...)

I don't like...

I don't like salad sandwiches
and I don't like garden peas!
I don't like sticky honey.
Who cares if it's made by bees?
I don't like Mummy's face
when she's searching for her keys.

I only like chocolate!

I don't like visiting hospital,
the wards are full of disease!
I don't like saying 'thank you'
and 'pardon me' and 'please'.
I don't like falling off my bike
and grazing my bare knees.

I only like chocolate.

I don't like Daddy's cooking,
it's everything with cheese.
I don't like Charlotte Reynolds,
she's the biggest, meanest tease.
I don't like Grandma's breathing,
when she splutters with a wheeze.

I only like chocolate!

I don't like bowls of porridge
or microwave meals for teas.
I don't like flying kites,
when the wind's a fragile breeze.
I don't like catching colds,
runny noses with a sneeze.

I only like chocolate.

I don't like winter mornings
and puddles all a freeze.
I don't like my new puppy.
Will he ever stop those wees?
I don't like homeless tomcats,
their coats are full of fleas.

I only like chocolate!

I don't like writing rhymes
and I've got nothing more to say.
So I'm going out with my friend Charlotte,
to the local park to play.

(Not THAT Charlotte, another one!)

My mum's secret Birthday cake

My mum deserved a birthday surprise!
I decided to make her a cake.
But dad forgot to turn on the oven
and the cake forgot to bake.

We dashed to the local supermarket,
as time was fading away.
I bought a birthday cake for my mum
to celebrate her day.

Mum arrived home from work,
looking tired, if you know what I mean.
'I've baked you a cake,' I shouted out.
'It's chocolate and jam and cream!'

'Thanks for baking this beautiful gift,'
she exclaimed with tears in her eyes.
I'm sure I'll tell her the truth one day,
as I know it's wrong to tell lies!

My dad

He's ace my dad!
And here's why:
My dad can fight any
wrestler in the whole world.

He's not scared of John Cena.
He's not scared of Roman Reigns.
He's not scared of Dean Ambrose.

He's not even scared of Randy Orton's
'RKO', whatever that stands for!

He's not scared of Ryback or Sin Cara.
He's not scared of the 'Big Show' or the
'Undertaker' **OR** the 'Rock' whoever he is.

Or the big fat one
with monster muscles.
Or the one with the
ugly face and long hair.
Or the one with huge tattoos
all over his thick arms.

MY DAD'S NOT SCARED OF ANY OF THEM,
THANK YOU VERY MUCH!
NOT ONE OF THEM!
NO HE'S NOT!

He tells me this:
'If any of those wrestling nerds
ever ANNOY me, Hannah,
I'll do this to them:

I'll pull down their shorts
I'll punch them in the nose.
I'll karate chop their arms.
I'll trip them up.
I'll call them silly names, like 'Fat face'!
I'll say you're ugly!
I'll say you smell like my granny's laundry!
I'll say your breath stinks!
I'll say you cry every time you fall over
in the school playground!
I'll say you can't even squash a grape!
I'll say you don't even know your 1x table!
I'll say you wear ladies perfume!
I'll say you wear pink underpants!

And I'll pull at their beards
UNTIL THEIR EYES WATER!

I love my dad!
He's big, strong and...
He's my SUPER-HERO!

But I've noticed one thing about him:

My dad only ever says all that stuff about
fighting wrestlers...
when he's watching them on my television.

Hold on, I know what you're thinking!

Well you're wrong because...

My dad's **REY MYSTERIO!**

So there!

*Nb 'RKO' stands for 'Randy Keith Orton'
or 'Randy's knock out'.*

Dentist Florence

In the shop on the corner
lived old Mr Keats,
selling a range of
various treats.
But one of his customers
was an international robber,
stealing chocolate and sweets
in a variety of clobber.

Chomp on my chocolate!
Crunch, crunch, munch!
Minty, melting chocolate!
Sugar for my lunch!

Dentist Florence's favourite
was a scrumptious snickers,
so she grabbed one off the counter
and stuffed it down her knickers.
She loved chocolate oranges,
foil wrapped in a box.
So she picked up three
and shoved them down her socks.

Chomp on my chocolate!
Crunch, crunch, munch!
Minty, melting chocolate!
Sugar for my lunch!

She picked up handfuls
of gobstoppers and chews,
stuffing them into
the sides of her shoes.
She scooped up spaceships
and chocolate rockets,
dropping them into her
over-sized pockets.

Chomp on my chocolate!
Crunch, crunch, munch!
Minty, melting chocolate!
Sugar for my lunch!

She found jelly babies,
in a see-through packet,
so she grabbed three bags
and hid them in her jacket.
She noticed an Easter egg,
wide and fat.
So she quickly disguised it,
under her hat.

Chomp on my chocolate!
Crunch, crunch, munch!
Minty, melting chocolate!
Sugar for my lunch!

She discovered a packet
of strawberry laces
but Mr Keats and his wife
wore angry faces.
'We know what you're up to!'
they shouted with a glare.
But Dentist Florence
didn't even care.

Chomp on my chocolate!
Crunch, crunch, munch!
Minty, melting chocolate!
Sugar for my lunch!

'Teeth rotters you're selling!'
she snapped like a croc,
grabbing an enormous
chocolate block.
'The amount of sugar
that's in this bar,
weighs as much
as a Landrover car!'

Chomp on my chocolate!
Crunch, crunch, munch!
Minty, melting chocolate!
Sugar for my lunch!

'Get out of my shop!'
Mr Keats cried out.
'I'm aware of the sugar;
of that I have no doubt.'
Dentist Florence screamed,
at the top of her voice:
'Too much sugar's a sin,
so repent, you have a choice!'

Chomp on my chocolate!
Crunch, crunch, munch!
Minty, melting chocolate!
Sugar for my lunch!

Dentist Florence marched off,
out onto the street.
She pulled out her Snickers,
her extra special treat.
As she chewed her chocolate,
she started a speech
about the dangerous places,
sugar can reach.

Chomp on my chocolate!
Crunch, crunch, munch!
Minty, melting chocolate!
Sugar for my lunch!

'Too much sugar causes
toothache and plaque.
And once a tooth's extracted,
you can never get it back!
We should all cut down on sugar
but I think it's only fair,
that DENTISTS AREN'T INCLUDED
so there; I don't care!'

Chomp on my chocolate!
Crunch, crunch, munch!
Minty, melting chocolate!
Sugar for my lunch!

Miss O'Hare's trumpathon

There's a smell around the carpet,
who could it be?
I don't think it's Abigail,
who's sitting next to me.

I don't think it's Thomas
or Seena or Sam
or Dominic or Freddie
or Mrs McCann.

I don't think it's Pippa
or Mia or Jane
or Harry or George
or that new boy, Hussein.

I have a strange feeling
it's Miss O'Hare,
reading our story
in her tall wooden chair.

She trumps a lot!
I've heard her before.
Twenty times last week,
well I'm keeping her score.

She trumps and trumps
and she blows off,
disguising the sound
with an innocent cough.

But whatever she does,
she can't hide the smell.
And she thinks us children
can't even tell.

But I know her secret,
I can tell by her face.
I know the mystery stinker,
polluting our space.

I don't have any evidence,
so she's always blaming me,
as her horrible smells
are impossible to see.

I'm fed up of her shouting,
'Olivia, is that you?'
and opening up the windows,
not one but a few.

So I've downloaded an app,
which shows you the name
of the trumper responsible,
the bottom to blame.

Tomorrow, it's story time,
so I'm going to switch it on
and hopefully I'll catch
her embarrassing trumpathon...

I pulled out my iPad
as she started 'Peace at last!'
And I waited on the carpet,
for her untimely, deadly blast.

She trumped like an elephant
and our classroom sort of shook.
So she buried her head
in her big picture book.

The smell drifted over
the carpet in our class.
And she poisoned thirty children,
with her thick, toxic gas.

And that's when she annoyed me,
something I would never do.
When she shouted loud and clear,
'Olivia, is that you?'

I tapped my iPad's app
and I screamed at Miss O'Hare.
'You're the one who's done it!
Blaming me; you're just not fair!'

My teacher's name appeared,
on my Apple iPad's screen.
And Miss O'Hare blushed,
with an angry, piercing scream.

She opened up the windows
and wafted out her fumes,
stronger than the laughing gas
in a thousand helium balloons.

I showed all the children,
who laughed with a roar
and Miss O'Hare vanished
through her classroom door.

We've never seen her since,
Mr Cain just says she's ill.
But I do miss her stories
and I think I always will.

I'm sure I'll see her one day.
I'll just have to wait and see.
But at least she'll NEVER ever again...

blame her trumps on me!

In trouble!

You can catch a ball but catch a cold
and you're in trouble!

You can run a bath but run a marathon
and you're in trouble!

You can crash a computer but crash a car
and you're in trouble!

You can drive a truck but drive your mum
MAD and you're in trouble!

You can start an engine but start a fight
and you're in trouble!

You can make a cake but make a mess
and you're in trouble!

You can miss a friend but miss a birthday
and you're in trouble!

You can crack a joke but crack a rib
and you're in trouble!

You can smash a world record but smash a
vase and you're in trouble!

You can burn a CD but burn your hand
and you're definitely...

IN TROUBLE!

Whatever happened to...

Whatever happened to my fleecy blanket?
Mum put it into a charity bag.

Whatever happened to my Jellycat turtle?
I lost it whilst on holiday in Spain.

Whatever happened to my best friend?
She moved house and changed schools.

Whatever happened to my favourite pen?
The ink dried up, so I threw it away.

Whatever happened to my old iPad?
I dropped it and smashed the screen.

Whatever happened to my old dog, Rusty?
He's chasing sticks in heaven now.

Whatever happened to my bouncy ball?
I bounced it too high and I lost it.

Whatever happened to my teddy bear, Zigbee?

He's still here and he'll never, ever leave me.

Old Uncle Tom bought him for me,
years and years and years ago.

I've cuddled up to Zigbee since I was born.

I talk to him every night.

He helps me to drift off to sleep.

I love Zigbee and Zigbee loves me.

And he'll always be my bestest friend
in the whole, wide world!

I LOVE YOU ZIGBEE!

xxXXXXX

Who's YOUR Zigbee?

Perhaps it was just a dream!

We have a new dinner lady,
who feeds on little children.
We call her the 'Hulk'
behind her back.

She stomps around the hall,
stealing our snacks,
munching on our cheddars
with her teeth stained black.

She steals our chocolates
and anything 'unhealthy'.
She's the demon confiscator,
a villain in disguise.

She's a 'five a day' expert,
a calculating crook,
scanning the hall
with her searchlight eyes.

'Give me those!'
she yelled last week,
grabbing Georgia's crisps
from her hand.

'I've told you before!
Am I talking to the wall?
ALL unhealthy snacks
have been banned!'

'You're just a big bully!'
I shouted out loud,
my heart,
an African drum.

'I know what happens
to the snacks you steal
and I'm gonna go home
and tell my mum!'

'Get to Sir's office!'
the Demon cried out,
shooting me a
razor sharp stare.

'The teachers make the rules
about unhealthy snacks,
so don't blame me;
it's not fair!'

I burst out crying
and strolled to Sir's office,
tripping up on
long, trailing laces.

My head crashed hard,
into the wall
and I couldn't recognise
teachers' faces.

Stars danced around
my aching head
and I thought I was
going to be sick.

'Ice-pack needed!'
somebody screamed.
'She's going to faint,
so be quick!'

Some teaching assistants
pulled me up
and they helped me
through a door.

I sat in the teachers' staffroom
and this is what I saw:

A huge tin of Cadbury's Roses.
A box of half empty Maltesers.
A tub of 'Rocky roads' from M&S.
A half eaten chocolate gateau.
A massive jar of Liquorice allsorts.
An enormous tin of Quality Street.
A giant box of Milk Tray.
Three Terry's chocolate oranges.
Several bags of 'Strawberry laces'
Numerous packets of Haribo sweets,
left over from the school disco, I think.

I've told my friends
about that fateful day,
the sweets, the chocolates
and the cream.

But the teachers say

I was *dazed* and *confused.*

So perhaps, it was

JUST A DREAM!

? ? ? ? ? ? ?

The digital age...

Everybody's living in the 'digital' age!
Even marmoset monkeys have iPads in their cage.
An apple's a computer and not a fruit
and online surfing's not a water pursuit.

A webpage sounds like a spider's in the house.
A hamster has a cage but computers have a mouse.
You can store gigabytes on your memory sticks
and access your data by several clicks.

An Xbox 360's a necessity!
It's arguably better than a PlayStation or Wii.
You might own a MacBook or a Kindle Firefox
or download an app for locating lost socks.

A hard-drive is nothing to do with a road.
But iPhone's are useless without a passcode.
An upload is something you can do to the cloud.
And if there's a thunderstorm, you'll still be allowed.

My grandad's desktop isn't made of wood.
He'd go back to chalkboards if he could.
He often says to me 'Just where will it end?'
Typing out an email, then clicking 'send'.

Files can be harmed by a virus or a bug.
They live in computers, not your mattress or your rug.
You don't even need a hospital bed...
just an anti-virus disk that'll clear your head!

Words change their meaning over the years.
Inventors dream up gadgets; blood, sweat and tears.
I wonder what I'll own when I'm ninety-three.
Perhaps a flying saucer but I'll have to wait and see!

I'm leaving school

Shaun's poem

I'm leaving school tomorrow!
Ha, ha, ha!
I won't be crying!
Ha, ha, ha!

I'll be hollering and cheering and singing and
dancing and laughing and giggling and
jumping and prancing.

Never again will Miss Clot shout my name,
picking on an innocent, somebody to blame.
Never again will old Clonk say 'That's wrong,'
strolling around like a born again King Kong.

I'm leaving school tomorrow!
Ha, ha, ha!
I won't be crying!
Ha, ha, ha!

I'll be hollering and cheering and singing and
dancing and laughing and giggling and
jumping and prancing.

Never again will I stand against that wall,
for talking in assembly, in the dining hall.
Never again will I lose my precious lunch,
for arguing and fighting, throwing a punch.

I'm leaving school tomorrow!
Ha, ha, ha!

I won't be crying!
Ha, ha, ha!

I'll be hollering and cheering and singing and
dancing and laughing and giggling and
jumping and prancing.

Never again will Mr Bore ring my mum,
blaming me for stuff that I haven't even done.
Never again will I have to do a test,
when I don't even care about trying my best.

I'm leaving school tomorrow!
Ha, ha, ha!
I won't be crying!
Ha, ha, ha!

I'll be hollering and cheering and singing and
dancing and laughing and giggling and
jumping and prancing.

I WON'T miss this school;
This is my final day .
So 'Get lost everybody!'
that's all I have to say.

Isobel's poem

I'm leaving school tomorrow!
Sob, sob, sob.
I'll definitely be crying!
Sob, sob, sob.

I'll be sobbing and shaking and spluttering
and screaming and weeping and howling
and thinking and dreaming.

Never again will Miss Size look after me,
sticking a plaster on my bleeding knee.
Never again will Miss Sharp give me a sticker,
For excellent work, not a crosser but a ticker.

I'm leaving school tomorrow!
Sob, sob, sob.
I'll definitely be crying!
Sob, sob, sob.

I'll be sobbing and shaking and spluttering
and screaming and weeping and howling
and thinking and dreaming.

Never again will I represent the school.
Hockey and netball, swimming in the pool.
Never again will a hug come from Miss,
soothing my sadness, like a Princess' kiss.

I'm leaving school tomorrow!
Sob, sob, sob.
I'll definitely be crying!
Sob, sob, sob.

I'll be sobbing and shaking and spluttering
and screaming and weeping and howling
and thinking and dreaming.

Never again will Miss Heyes ask how I feel.
She knows I'm Mum's carer, a hamster on a wheel.
Never again will Mr Redfern miss his break,
working in his playtime, all for my sake.

I'm leaving school tomorrow!
Sob, sob, sob.
I'll definitely be crying!
Sob, sob, sob.

I'll be sobbing and shaking and spluttering
and screaming and weeping and howling
and thinking and dreaming.

I'll REALLY miss MY school;
This is my final day .
So 'Thank you to my teachers,'
that's all I have to say.

Mr Jameson's groovy school uniform

Monday:
Black trousers, white shirt, pink tie.
'Rudolph' Christmas socks.
(Worn at any time of the year!)

Tuesday:
The same as above but 'disguised' with a
grey crew neck pullover over the top.
'Best Grandad in the world' socks.
(Only if the Rudolph socks are sweaty!)

Wednesday: (PE day)
Blue Adidas tracksuit, Slazenger polo shirt
and white flannel socks.

Thursday:
Beige trousers, blue shirt, annoying brown
tie with gorilla picture on the front.
'World's best teacher' socks.

Friday:
Grey pants, white shirt, favourite blue tie
with hypnotic pattern on the front.
Grey tank top. (Even in summer!)
'Happy Halloween' green and black socks.
(Again, worn at any time of the year!)

Saturday:
n/a (Not applicable)

Sunday:
Loungewear set
(On computer / marking books all day long)

Monday:
Go back to Monday on the other page...

PS
There's probably somebody like
Mr Jameson hanging around your school.
See if you can spot him!
He might even be YOUR teacher...

Mrs Lawrence's supermarket trolley

I saw her the other day, in the supermarket.
My teaching assistant, Mrs Lawrence.
She didn't notice me.
I was hiding behind my nana and Grandad.
I looked into Mrs Lawrence's trolley.
And this is what I saw:

One bag of pick and mix, expertly weighed.
Two litre bottles of fizzy lemonade.
Three Strawberry trifles, covered in cream.
Four Belgian waffles, a sugary dream.
Five tins of maple syrup, thicker than oil.
Six Cadbury's cream eggs, wrapped in foil.
Seven chocolate rabbits, fresh from a mould.
Eight big boxes of Terry's 'All gold'.
Nine big bags of Haribo treats.
Ten small packets of various sweets.

A few days later, a science lesson loomed.
We had a new topic, all about teeth.
Mrs Lawrence helped Miss Griffiths teach us some fun and interesting facts:
All about **looking after your teeth.**

'Sugar is a dangerous substance,'
Mrs Lawrence snapped. 'I know it tastes nice, of course BUT cut it out of your diet RIGHT NOW, or you're asking for trouble.

Your teeth will turn black and you'll have a mouth full of horrible, silver fillings.
And your teeth will all fall out – probably when you're all in Y6, during SAT's week!'

'YOU have been warned!'
barked Miss Griffiths.

'Yes, YOU have been warned!'
added Mrs Lawrence.

'THEY have been warned!'
repeated Miss Griffiths.

'Yes, THEY have been warned,'
repeated Mrs Lawrence.

'Err excuse me, Mrs Lawrence,' I said.
'But I'm sure I saw you in the supermarket at the weekend and your trolley was, well, full of sugar. In fact, I suppose you could call it an enormous, sweet and sugar mountain.'

Mrs Lawrence's eyes enlarged.
Two huge golf balls stared out at me, piercing my forehead like strong, powerful laser beams.

Her face erupted like a vicious and violent volcano, her skin bubbling up.

Tiny blood vessels almost burst, creating a round and red pulsating, beetroot face.

She cracked her trembling knuckles.
She rolled those golf ball eyes around in their sockets, all sunken in thick and spongy fat.

'Oh, Abigail,' she said,
stretching her lips into a wry smile.

'That's my identical twin sister you're talking about!
You can't tell us apart.
She's in love with sugar.
In fact, she's a bit of an addict.'

'Oh,' I said.

Peter's brother

He said he was a cannibal,
Peter's brother.
It runs in the family,
as so was his mother.
She ate Peter's teacher
one day for tea,
with mashed potatoes
and thick gravy.

Peter ate the caretaker,
fried in batter.
The school didn't open
but it didn't really matter.
'Where's Mr Jones?
He's never ever late.'
But the teachers didn't know
he'd disappeared on Peter's plate!

Peter's mum took a
fancy to a Year 4 teacher.
She arranged a meeting,
so that she could see her.
'Peter doesn't listen,'
Miss Clarkson said.
'Everything I say
goes over his head!'

'You're picking on my boy!'
Peter's mum cried out.
'That's what this silly
meeting's all about!'
'He's a pain!' said Miss Fletcher.
'Who just loves to disrupt.'
So Peter's hungry mum
simply gobbled her up.

The head-teacher, Mrs Kearney,
waltzed into the room.
'Have you seen Miss Clarkson?
It's her Science afternoon.
She's working on changes
like evaporation
and freezing materials
and condensation.'

'I know a bit of science,'
said Peter's mum.
'I love investigations,
they're so much fun!
I can give you an example
of irreversible change.
It's a bit like melting
but sort of rearranged.'

'I hope your test is fair,'
the head teacher announced.
'Not really!' Peter's mum said,
as she suddenly pounced.
'This change is irreversible,
it will make you thinner!'
And biting Mrs Kearney,
she tucked into her dinner.

Arrgghh!!

Merton Bank Primary School (St Helens)

WANTED FOR SEPTEMBER

Head teacher
1 teacher for Key stage 1 (Infant)
1 teacher for Key stage 2 (Junior)
Caretaker

If you've enjoyed the poetry in this book,
you'll LOVE Paul's first poetry book:

Here are two lovely poems from 'I'm fed up!'

I wonder...

I wonder what a goldfish thinks about,
swimming in a bowl.
Is he dreaming of a bigger tank
or a long lost family shoal?

Is he waiting for another fish
to share his watery home?
Or is he happy all alone,
King of his own glass dome?
I wonder...

I wonder what a parrot thinks about, sitting in a cage.
Is she happy talking and squawking, a performer on a stage.

Is she dreaming of her jungle, longing to stretch her wings?

Or is her spirit fading, forgetting what freedom brings.

I wonder…

I wonder what a brown bear thinks about, dancing in the street.

Is he happy on his chain, skipping to the beat?

Is he dreaming of a mountain, a forest or a meadow?

Or praying for a future and a better tomorrow?

I wonder…

I wonder what an old lady thinks about, sitting in her chair.

Is she happy in her home, smiling with a stare?

Is she recalling her husband, their perfect wedding day?

Or remembering her friends, who've sadly passed away.

I wonder…

Audrey and Claude

Two baby elephants, Audrey and Claude,
went for a swim at the baths.
They jumped and dived and splashed in the water,
which was fun and a lot of laughs.

'I've had enough!' a lifeguard screamed.
'Please climb out of the pool!
You two naughty animals
have broken an important rule!'

'Why what's up?' asked Audrey.
'We haven't done anything wrong.'
The lifeguard stared and shouted out,
'your trunks are far too long!'

Here's a poem from 'My favourite trainers' –
poetry for older children, teenagers and adults.

A bird with a broken wing

I discovered a bird today,
a bird with a broken wing.

Pain and shock was invading his body,
but he continued to sing.

He fluttered his shattered feathers,
desperately trying to fly.

But in my hands his spirit was fading
as he dreamed of flying high.

Perhaps he flew into a lamppost.
Perhaps he flew into a tree.

Perhaps a tomcat pounced on him,
hungry for his tea.

Perhaps he crashed into a windscreen,
a car travelling too fast.

But in my hands, he gazed into my eyes
and then he breathed his last.

Paul Delaney

My favourite trainers!
Poetry

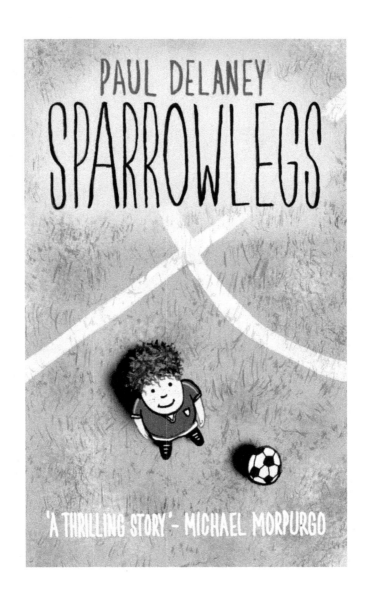

THE MAGICAL & MYSTERIOUS

MADAME MISTRAL

PAUL DELANEY

'Sometimes, I've believed
as many as six impossible
things before breakfast...'

LEWIS CARROL

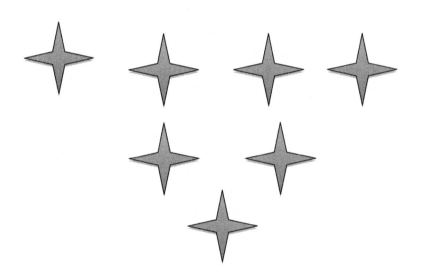

'So come with me, where dreams are born and time is never planned. Just think of happy things and your heart will fly on wings. Forever, in Never Never Land.'

J.M. Barrie (1860 – 1937)

Creator of Peter Pan

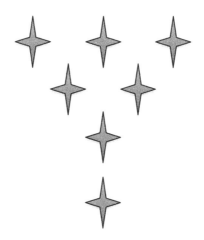

Index of the second set of '44'

The end

There are NO other poems in this book!

Lightning Source UK Ltd.
Milton Keynes UK
UKOW04f1409111117
312515UK00001B/183/P